Little Stories for Little Readers

Beginning Reproducible Books
in English and Spanish

dog

perro

by: Susan M. Ketch

Craig Johnson

Joy Gornto

Carson-Dellosa Publishing Company, Inc.
Greensboro, NC

Credits

Editor:	Kelly Gunzenhauser
Art Coordinator:	Erik Huffine
Layout Design:	Jon Nawrocik
Inside Illustrations:	Mike Duggins
	Julie Kinlaw
	Ray Lambert
	Wayne Miller
	Bill Neville
Cover Design:	Annette Hollister-Papp
Cover Illustrations:	Julie Kinlaw
	Dan Sharp

ISBN 1-59441-150-6

Table of Contents

© Carson-Dellosa   Little Stories for Little Readers • CD-104046

Introduction and Ideas for Using These Books

Introduction

Many teachers work with bright, eager students who are willing to learn and happy to be in school, but can only speak a few words of English. Many parents of English-speaking children send them to school hoping that they will get a chance to learn another language. There are also students from both groups who are just beginning to read or who have been trying to learn for a long time. And of course, there is always that additional, unwelcome "member" of the classroom, the budget that limits the number of books teachers and families can purchase. *Little Stories for Little Readers* addresses all of these issues!

In this book are 12 reproducible stories that roughly correspond to most emergent readers' levels three and four. Each story is illustrated with simple, yet clever, black-and-white art that is perfect for coloring. Also, each story is repeated with the same plot, characters, and illustrations, but is translated into Spanish. To use this book, simply copy enough stories for each student to have one, let students cut apart the pages and color the illustrations, then choose a method for students to bind them together. Each story has an accompanying activity page that addresses different reading and language skills. When students are finished assembling the books and completing the corresponding lessons, let them take the books home to add to their personal libraries. Also, plan to keep a copy of each book in your classroom library.

Making the Books

Many reproducible books involve complicated copying, folding, and cutting. However, *Little Stories for Little Readers* pays special attention to ease of use for young students and busy teachers. To make one book, copy the book pages single-sided. Have the student color each page of the book, then have her cut the pages in half on the dashed lines. (Coloring before cutting and binding makes the coloring easier.) Finally, have each student turn the pages in the same direction, check that they are in the correct order, and staple them on the left side. Help students with stapling so that their books open easily. Students can also bind the pages using a hole punch and yarn or metal rings. When class time is at a premium, send home bookmaking instructions so that families can help students make the books at home.

Special Coloring and Other Bookmaking Instructions

Encourage students to be as creative as possible when making the books so that each book will be unique and valuable to its owner. Follow these tips to entice students to become book illustrators of the finest order. And remember, with any type of coloring other than crayon or colored pencil, let books dry completely before allowing students to assemble the pages.

- If desired, enlarge book pages before making class sets so that students can color them more easily. For the classroom library, consider enlarging the pages to big-book size.

- Students will enjoy using materials other than crayons to color their books. Let them use paint (especially watercolor), markers, glitter glue, colored pencils, etc. Also, gear students' art media to special needs for different books. For example, students might enjoy using glitter to make the snowflakes in the *Weather* book (page 53) while they may feel that the landscape in *I Live on a Farm* (page 84) lends itself to watercolor.

- Not all children's book illustrations are in color. Some students may enjoy the challenge of coloring in pencil and using different shades of gray and patterns to distinguish areas. Provide some sample books that are illustrated in black and white, such as books by Chris Van Allsburg, before students attempt this exercise.

- Use torn tissue paper and watered-down glue to let students create collages in their books. (Students must have well-developed fine motor skills for this to work well.) This technique may require enlarging pages to big-book size or only using books with larger expanses of background, such as *I Live on a Farm* (page 84).

- If the budget permits, copy the book onto different types of paper, such as construction paper, pastel typing paper, textured paper, etc. Set aside a few blank pages for students to try out different art techniques. They will enjoy seeing how different media look on different types of paper.

- Let students be creative when binding the books. If students are careful, they can punch holes in the books and use string, yarn, fabric, or metal rings to bind them.

- Create a class book in a unique way. Enlarge a book and then copy the pages onto transparencies. Provide write-on/wipe-away markers and let students take turns coloring the pages on the overhead projector. Let each student color one page, then read the book as a class.

- Make a class set of books for students to share. Copy, cut apart, and laminate the pages. Bind the pages with metal rings. Store the books at a center with write-on/wipe-away markers. Allow students to visit the center to color the books. Provide paper towels so that each student may erase the previous student's work before coloring a book.

- Use the blank page template (page 124) to let students write and illustrate their own stories. Each week, feature a different student's original story by allowing him to read it to the class. Let more proficient readers and writers do this earlier in the year so that less-skilled writers have a chance to improve before they become guest authors.

- Use books for more than just reading practice. Provide tracing paper and let students trace the illustrations. This will improve their drawing abilities and fine motor skills.

Using the Books with Students

In addition to filling out your classroom library, these books can serve a variety of purposes. Students can make and take home up to 24 different books if both language versions are used, which can significantly increase some students' personal libraries. Spanish speakers will feel good about reading books on the same level as their English-speaking classmates. Students who speak primarily English or Spanish can broaden their vocabularies and increase their fluency. And, best of all, students will have access to more quality readers. Use any or all of the following activities to incorporate Little Stories into your classroom.

- Help a new Spanish speaker feel welcome in an English-speaking classroom by making him a guest reader. Let the student choose one of the stories to share with the class. Have the class color, cut out, and bind both versions of the story. Allow the guest reader to practice reading the story to you or a partner until he feels comfortable. Then, read the English version aloud to the class and let the student read the Spanish version. Explain that his reading is meant to be an example for how native Spanish speakers sound. Then, let other students meet in small groups to chorally read the story in Spanish, following the example of the native speaker.

- Reading in a new language is as easy as ABC! Use the books to teach the English and Spanish alphabet. Assign a story that has several letters in common between the two versions. Have each student color, cut out, and assemble the books. Then, have students use colored pencil to go on a scavenger hunt looking for the assigned letters. Write some of the words on the board and talk about the different sounds the letters make in both languages. Be sure to point out the letters that appear in only the Spanish alphabet (ch, ll, ñ, rr), where appropriate. (Note that some Spanish speakers no longer include some of these as separate letters in their alphabet.)

- Choose a story to teach new words. Give the Spanish version to English speakers and vice versa. Provide a copy of the glossary (page 126) for each student. Let students underline unfamiliar words in colored pencil and look up those words in the glossary, then color and cut out the books. Have students create mini-dictionaries for their books on the blank backs of the last pages of their books. Add additional pages if necessary using the blank page template (page 124). Set aside time for students to study and learn the new words. Then, let each student bring her book to your desk. Read the story with her and ask her what each underlined word means.

- Have a magic word reading. For this activity, provide English books for native Spanish speakers and Spanish books for English speakers. Explain that you will read the story in students' non-native language. Then, choose an important word from the story, talk about it in the native language, and have students try to guess which non-native word corresponds to the native word as you read. For example, for Spanish speakers in the story *School Stuff,* choose a word like *nuevo* (*new*) and see if students can guess which word it might be as you read the story in English.

- Practice fluency in any language. Enlarge a story or copy it onto transparencies. Share it aloud with the class in both languages. Then, let students make their mini-books. Assign half of the class to read in English and the other half to read in Spanish. Have a class read-aloud time. As you show the pages in your copy, let students chorally read along in their assigned languages, taking turns for every page. Then, let pairs of students continue practicing together in the same way. When students are fluent in their assigned languages, have them swap books. Repeat the class choral reading and the pair practice until students are fluently reading the story in both languages.

Little Stories for Little Readers • CD-104046

- Partner reading in two languages can be fun. Pair a fluent English reader with a fluent Spanish reader. Have the partners agree on one story they would both like to turn into a book. Let the Spanish reader color the English book and let the English reader color the Spanish book. Then, instruct students to swap books and read aloud to each other. Tell students to pay careful attention to how their partners are reading because they will be reading in their non-native languages next. When students have heard the story read aloud, let them swap books and read in their non-native languages. Have the English reader coach the Spanish reader on her English pronunciation and reading, and let the Spanish reader coach the English reader on his Spanish pronunciation. Finally, let both students read their story aloud to the class. Compliment each pair on something, such as teamwork, pronunciation, general fluency, expression, etc.

- Students benefit from hearing their reading improve. Use a tape recorder to help students practice reading the stories in either language. Have a student record herself reading a story for the first time. Let her practice it four times, then record it a second time. After the second recording, let the student listen to both of her readings to demonstrate that practice does make perfect.

- Let Spanish- and English-speaking students use their native languages to improve their expression when reading in non-native languages. Allow each student to practice reading a story fluently in his native language (English or Spanish) and then record himself. Work with the student on his expression while reading. Then, have him play back the recording and talk with him about positive aspects of his reading. Next, let the student record himself reading the story in his non-native language, attempting to recreate the same expression and fluency he used in the first, native reading. Compare the two readings and make additional assignments according to the student's individual needs.

- Choose a different pair of stories for students to use to make books each week. After the books are made, select vocabulary from the stories and have a bilingual spelling bee. Assign students a list of Spanish and English words from the story. Refer them to the glossary (page 126) for definitions. Then, have a spelling bee. Divide the class into two teams. Try to assign an equal number of native English and Spanish speakers to each team. Call out the words randomly in either English or Spanish. For example, for the story *Las arañas*, give the first student in line for Team A the word *arañas* (*spiders*) to spell, define, give the English equivalent of, etc. If the student is correct, give that team a point. If the student is incorrect, allow Team B to spell, define, or give the English equivalent for a point. Alternate between Spanish and English words for both teams. The team with the most points at the end of the game wins. As a reward, let the winning team choose the story for the next spelling bee.

Let's Eat Ice Cream!

Susan M. Ketch

Level 3
Number of English Words: 33
Number of Spanish Words: 37

Pre-Reading Activities

Book Introduction: Tell students that the family in this book likes to eat ice cream.

Discussion Suggestions: Ask, "Do you like to eat ice cream? What is your favorite flavor? What are the favorite flavors of other people in your family?"

Picture Walk: Point out the ice cream parlor (heladería) and ask if students have a special place to get ice cream in their neighborhoods. Let students decide, based on the pictures, what kinds of ice cream they think the family members in the story choose. Ask students to describe what the different kinds of ice cream they name look like.

Word Work:
Punctuation—Point out and name quotation marks, exclamation points, and commas. Structure—Point out that *"'Oh yes!' said _____."* and *"¡Sí, qué rico!"* are recurring patterns.

Post-Reading Questions

1. Who got ice cream in the story?
2. Did each person get the same kind of ice cream?
3. How do you know the family likes ice cream?

Extension Activities

1. Provide letter manipulatives for *w, e, h, m,* and *b.* Make the word *we.* Then, change the first letter to an *m.* Ask, "What is the new word you have made? Can you change the first letter again and make a new word?"
2. Tell students, "Think about the kinds of foods you like to eat. List or draw your favorite foods on a piece of paper to make a menu."
3. Ask each child to tell you her favorite ice cream flavor. Make a graph. Which is the most popular flavor?

Related Literature

- *Benny Bakes a Cake* by Eve Rice (Greenwillow, 1993)
- *Let's Find Out about Ice Cream* by Mary Ebeltoft Reid (Scholastic, 1997)
- *Wemberly's Ice Cream Star* by Kevin Henkes (HarperFestival, 2003)

Translation Notes

¡Qué rico! means *"How delicious!" Rico* can also mean *rich* or *wealthy.*

Note the difference between the words used for *Mom, Dad, Grandmother,* and *Grandfather,* and the words *Mamá, Papá, Abuelito,* and *Abuelita.*

Little Stories for Little Readers • CD-104046

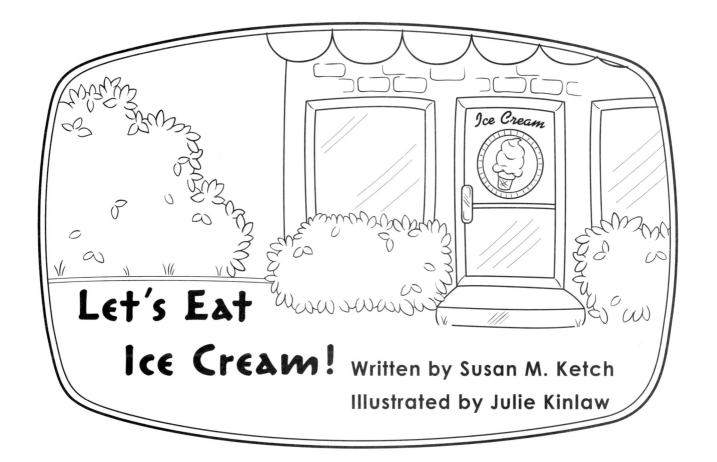

Let's Eat Ice Cream!

Written by Susan M. Ketch

Illustrated by Julie Kinlaw

Dad said, "Let's eat ice cream!"

"Oh, yes!" said Mom.

"Oh, yes!" said Rose.

"Oh, yes!" said Martin.

"Oh, yes!" said Grandmother.

"Oh, yes!" said Grandfather.

"We all like to eat ice cream!"

¡Qué rico helado!

Escrito por Susan M. Ketch

Ilustrado por Julie Kinlaw

¡Vamos a comer helado! —dijo Papá.

¡Sí, qué rico! —dijo Mamá.

¡Sí, qué rico! —dijo Rosita.

¡Sí, qué rico! —dijo Martincito.

¡Sí, qué rico! —dijo Abuelita.

¡Sí, qué rico! —dijo Abuelito.

¡A todos nos gusta comer helado!

Be Nice to Animals

Craig Johnson

Level 3
Number of English Words: 58
Number of Spanish Words: 36

Pre-Reading Activities

Book Introduction: This book tells and shows how to be nice to animals.

Discussion Suggestions: Ask, "Why should we be nice to animals? Do you have pets? Have you seen any of the animals in this book?" Graph how many students have pets and what kinds they have.

Picture Walk: As students see the pictures, ask them to name each animal they recognize.

Word Work:
Sight words—Students should learn to sight read *I, see, dog, cat, be,* and *the.*
Structure—Point out that *I see a _____.*
Be nice to the _____ is a recurring pattern.
Also note the patterns in *Veo un _____* and *Cuida al _____.*

Post-Reading Activities

1. Ask students how to be nice to classroom pets. Let students demonstrate kind behavior to stuffed animals.
2. Talk about different animals and the sounds they make, then sing "Old MacDonald Had a Farm." Ask students to name some animals they can't hear, such as worms and fish.
3. Invite a veterinarian to visit the classroom and talk about kind pet care.

Extension Activities

1. Have each student write or dictate sentences about an animal he has been nice to. Let students draw self-portraits with the animals they describe.
2. Play a game called Which Animals? Ask, "Which animals have six legs? Which animals have spots? Which animals have feathers?" Categorize and list answers on the board.
3. Pantomime and mimic animals and let students guess which animals you are imitating.

Related Literature

- *Dear Mr. Blueberry* by Simon James (Aladdin, 1996)
- *Henry and Mudge and the Happy Cat* by Cynthia Rylant (Aladdin, 1996)
- *Martha Speaks* by Susan Meddaugh (Houghton Mifflin, 1995)

Translation Notes

The Spanish animal names change slightly by taking on the *-ito* ending, which makes the words mean *little animals.* For example, *perro* means *dog,* whereas *perrito* means *little dog, young dog,* or *puppy.* The *-ito* ending is used here as a term of endearment.

Little Stories for Little Readers • CD-104046

Be Nice to Animals

Written by Craig Johnson   **Illustrated by Ray Lambert**

I see a dog. Be nice to the dog.

I see a cat. Be nice to the cat.

I see a bird. Be nice to the bird.

I see a rabbit. Be nice to the rabbit.

I see a fish. Be nice to the fish.

I see a lot of animals. Be nice to all of the animals!

Be Nice to Animals • CD-104046 • © Carson-Dellosa

6

Cuida los animales

Escrito por Craig Johnson   **Ilustrado por Ray Lambert**

Veo un perro. Cuida al perrito.

Veo un gato. Cuida al gatito.

Veo un pájaro. Cuida al pajarito.

Veo un conejo. Cuida al conejito.

Veo un pez. Cuida al pececito.

Veo muchos animales. ¡Cuídalos a todos!

Don't Make a Mess, Tess!

Craig Johnson

Level 3
Number of English Words: 50
Number of Spanish Words: 58

Pre-Reading Activities

Book Introduction: In this book, Tess's mom dad, sister, and brother tell Tess not to make a mess. Ask, "Do you think she makes a mess anyway?" Record students' predictions.

Discussion Suggestions: Ask, "Do you ever make a mess? Is anyone messy at your house? Who cleans up the mess?"

Picture Walk: For each picture, have students identify the objects Tess uses to make a mess.

Word Work:
Punctuation—Have students point out exclamation points and quotation marks.
Sight words—Students should learn to sight read *my, mom, said, to, me, a,* and *I.*
Word analogies—Compare the sounds of the words *Tess* and *mess,* and *Consuelo* and *suelo.*
Structure—Point out that *My _____ said (to me),* "*Don't make a mess, Tess.*" is a recurring pattern. Also note the patterns in *Mi _____ me dijo: —¡Consuelo, no tires las cosas al suelo!*

Post-Reading Activities

1. Ask, "Who makes a mess at your house?" Have each student draw a mess he or someone else made in his house. Ask, "Is the youngest person always the messiest?"
2. Have a class cleanup day with students. Store materials, clean surfaces, wash boards, and organize desks.

Independent Activities

1. Have students talk, write, or draw about Tess's next mess or about what may happen next in the story.
2. Make a "mess" by scattering picture cards and let students "clean" by sorting them.
3. Have each student write one chore she could do at home on an index card. Send cards home and have families sign and return them when students have helped with the chores.

Related Literature

- *The Berenstain Bears and the Messy Room* by Stan and Jan Berenstain (Random House, 1983)
- *Messy Bessey* by Patricia and Fredrick McKissack (Children's Press, 2000)
- *Mr. Messy* by Roger Hargreaves (Price Stern Sloan, 1998)
- *No, David!* by David Shannon (Scholastic, 1998)

Translation Notes

In the Spanish version, the name *Tess* is changed to *Consuelo* to rhyme with *suelo,* the Spanish word for *floor* or *ground.* The Spanish words for *mess* are *tiradero, relajo,* and *alboroto. No tires las cosas al suelo* literally means *Do not throw things on the floor.* This translation was chosen to match the rhyming pattern in the English version.

Little Stories for Little Readers • CD-104046

Don't Make a Mess, Tess!

Written by Craig Johnson

Illustrated by Bill Neville

My mom said to me, "Don't make a mess, Tess!"

My dad said, "Don't make a mess, Tess!"

My sister said to me, "Don't make a mess, Tess!"

My brother said, "Don't make a mess, Tess!"

Everybody said to me, "Don't make a mess, Tess!"

Oops! I made a mess!

¡Consuelo, no tires las cosas al suelo!

Escrito por Craig Johnson

Ilustrado por Bill Neville

Mi mamá me dijo:
—¡Consuelo, no tires las cosas al suelo!

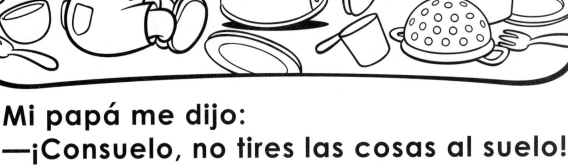

Mi papá me dijo:
—¡Consuelo, no tires las cosas al suelo!

Mi hermana me dijo:
—¡Consuelo, no tires las cosas al suelo!

Mi hermano me dijo:
—¡Consuelo, no tires las cosas al suelo!

Todos me dijeron:
—¡Consuelo, no tires las cosas al suelo!

¡Ay! Ya las tiré.

My New Puppy

Joy Gornto

Level 3
Number of English Words: 48
Number of Spanish Words: 30

Pre-Reading Activities

Book Introduction: This book is about what a new puppy does for fun.

Discussion Suggestions: Ask, "Have you ever had a puppy? What do puppies like to do?"

Picture Walk: As you show the pictures, ask what the puppy is doing. Ask if some of the things are good or bad to do, or just normal for new puppies.

Word Work:
Sight words—Students should learn to sight read *my, is, on,* and *the.*
Word analogies—Compare the sound of the word *my* to other familiar long /i/ words that end with the letter *y.*
Structure—Point out that *My new puppy* and *Mi perrito* are recurring patterns.

Post-Reading Activities

1. Discuss rhymes with students. Ask if students can think of rhyming words for *red, not,* and *cat.* Write correct responses on the board. Then, point out and discuss rhyming words in the story.
2. Talk about the responsibility of getting a new pet. Brainstorm a list of things a new pet needs, such as attention, a bed or cage, food, and water.

Independent Activities

1. Have students look in the book for words that rhyme with *me* and *sun.*
2. Tell each student to write or dictate a sentence about something a puppy might do. Let students illustrate their sentences and share them with the class.
3. With administrative and families' permission, have a volunteer bring a puppy to the classroom. Photograph students with the puppy. Have students draw pictures and send thank-you notes to the owner.

Related Literature

- *A Dog Named Sam* by Janice Boland (Puffin, 1998)
- *Just Me and My Puppy* by Mercer Mayer (Bt Bound, 2001)
- *The Puppy Who Wanted a Boy* by Jane Thayer (HarperCollins, 2003)

Translation Notes

Perro is the Spanish word for *dog. Perrito* means *small dog* or *puppy.*

The word *new* was eliminated from the translation to create a better rhyme scheme.

The Spanish word for *door* is *puerta. Biting on the door* is translated as *biting here* to rhyme with *pipí.*

On page 5 in the Spanish version, *ya está dormido* means *is already asleep.*

Little Stories for Little Readers • CD-104046

My New Puppy

Written by Joy Gornto

Illustrated by Mike Duggins

My new puppy is chewing on the soap.

My new puppy is pulling on the rope.

My new puppy is wetting on the floor.

My new puppy is biting on the door.

My new puppy is sleeping on the ground.

My new puppy is fun to have around!

Mi perrito

Escrito por Joy Gornto

Ilustrado por Mike Duggins

Mi perrito se come el jabón.

Mi perrito tira del cordón.

Mi perrito se hace pipí.

Mi perrito muerde aquí.

Mi perrito ya está dormido.

Mi perrito es muy divertido.

Scribbles

Susan M. Ketch

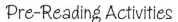

Level 3

Number of English Words: 38

Number of Spanish Words: 35

Pre-Reading Activities

Book Introduction: Scribbles is the name of a guinea pig who is a class pet.

Discussion Suggestions: Ask, "Does our classroom have a pet? What is its name? Can anyone tell us about guinea pigs?"

Picture Walk: Ask what Scribbles is doing on each page. Talk about the phrases *he likes* and *le gusta.*

Word Work:

Sight words—Students should learn to sight read *he, likes,* and *to.*

Word analogies—Compare the sound of the word *to* to another sight word such as *do.* Compare the word *he* to other sight words such as *we* and *me.*

Structure—Point out that *He likes to* and *Le gusta* are recurring patterns.

Post-Reading Questions

1. Ask, "Without rereading the story, can you tell how many things Scribbles did?"
2. Ask, "What other animals are like Scribbles?" Students may say hamsters, gerbils, etc.
3. Ask, "Why do you think the children like to see Scribbles?"

Independent Activities

1. Tell students to write or dictate and illustrate stories about the class pet or pets they have at home.
2. Ask students what kinds of pets they have. Graph students' pets and discuss the most popular and most unusual pets.
3. Let each student design a new home for Scribbles. Make sure students include places for food, water, sleeping, playing, and a way to watch him.

Related Literature

- *Frederick* by Leo Lionni (Dragonfly, 1973)
- *The Guinea Pig: An Owner's Guide to a Happy, Healthy Pet* by Audrey Pavia (Howell Book House, 1997)

Translation Notes

There are many infinitives in the story. Spanish verbs that end with *-ar, -er,* and *-ir* are in their infinitive forms.

Little Stories for Little Readers • CD-104046

Scribbles

Written by Susan M. Ketch
Illustrated by Bill Neville

Scribbles is a guinea pig. He lives in my classroom.

He likes to eat.

He likes to drink.

He likes to sleep.

He likes to play.

He likes to see the children.

The children like to see him.

Garabato

Escrito por Susan M. Ketch

Ilustrado por Bill Neville

Garabato es un cobaya. Garabato vive en mi salón.

Le gusta comer.

Le gusta beber.

Le gusta dormir.

Le gusta jugar.

Le gusta ver a los niños.

Garabato • CD-104046 • © Carson-Dellosa

**A los niños les gusta
ver a Garabato.**

Garabato • CD-104046 • © Carson-Dellosa

Weather

Susan M. Ketch

Level 3
Number of English Words: 59
Number of Spanish Words: 46

Pre-Reading Activities

Book Introduction: This is a book about the different kinds of weather that can happen during the year.

Discussion Suggestions: Ask, "What kinds of weather do you like best? What clothes do you wear on a snowy day? On a sunny, warm day? On a rainy day?"

Picture Walk: As you show the pictures, ask, "What clues do you see in the pictures that help you know what kind of weather it is?" Guide students to notice how the weather affects the kinds of activities the children do.

Word Work:
Sight words—Students should learn to sight read *it, is, a,* and *day.*
Word analogies—Compare the sounds of the words *it* and *is.*
Structure—Point out that *It is a _____ day.*
It is _____ outside is a recurring pattern.
Also note the patterns in *Es un día _____* and *¡Qué _____!*

Post-Reading Questions

1. Ask, "How many different kinds of weather did you read about?"
2. Ask, "What are some problems weather can cause?" Discuss flooding, hurricanes, tornadoes, etc.

3. Ask, "Which weather usually happens in summer? In winter?" Discuss how local weather compares to a four-seasons pattern.

Independent Activities

1. Have a volunteer mark the morning calendar with an *R* for rainy, *S* for sunny, *W* for windy, *C* for cloudy, or *SN* for snowy.
2. Let students make collages from magazine pictures of different kinds of weather.
3. Tell students that when the weather is cold, they usually eat warm foods. When the weather is hot, they usually eat cool foods. Have pairs brainstorm warm and cool foods.

Related Literature

- *The Cloud Book* by Tomie dePaola (Holiday House, 1985)
- *Down Comes the Rain* by Franklyn M. Branley (HarperTrophy, 1997)
- *The Wind Blew* by Pat Hutchins (Aladdin, 1993)

Translation Notes

Weather comes every day is translated here as *Every day the weather is different* to be more correct as a Spanish idiom.

It is is translated as *qué,* which means *how* when used in an exclamation. For example, *¡Qué frío!* means *How cold!* The same wording is used in *¡Qué rico helado!* (the Spanish version of *Let's Eat Ice Cream!*).

Little Stories for Little Readers • CD-104046

Weather

Written by Susan M. Ketch

Illustrated by Julie Kinlaw

It is a sunny day. It is nice outside.

It is a cloudy day. It is dark outside.

It is a windy day. It is messy outside.

It is a rainy day. It is wet outside.

It is a snowy day. It is cold outside.

It can be a hot day or a cold day.

Weather comes every day.

El tiempo

Escrito por Susan M. Ketch

Ilustrado por Julie Kinlaw

Es un día soleado. ¡Qué lindo!

Es un día nublado. ¡Qué oscuro!

Es un día con viento. ¡Qué alboroto!

Es un día lluvioso. ¡Qué mojado!

Es un día con nieve. ¡Qué frío!

Hay días de calor y días de frío.

Cada día el tiempo es diferente.

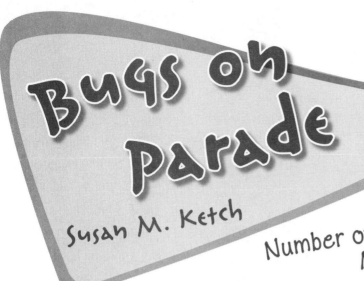

Bugs on Parade

Susan M. Ketch

Level 4
Number of English Words: 32
Number of Spanish Words: 27

Pre-Reading Activities

Book Introduction: Explain that this book is about different kinds of insects. In this book, they are called bugs.

Discussion Suggestions: Ask, "What bugs do you see around your houses? What kinds of bugs are your favorites and why?"

Picture Walk: As students look through the book, talk about each type of bug and ask if students know what kind of bug is shown. Which bugs have students seen?

Word Work:
Sight words—Students should learn to sight read *here, is,* and *a.* Point out and name the color words.
Word analogies—Have students think of words that rhyme with *bug.*
Structure—Note that *Here is a _____ bug* and *Este insecto es* are recurring patterns.

Post-Reading Activities

1. Ask, "How many bugs did you see?"
2. Ask students to name some problems bugs cause and some good things bugs do.

Independent Activities

1. Provide letter manipulatives to spell both *bug* and *insecto.* Let each student make these words. Have him make the word *bug* while reading the English version and *insecto* while reading the Spanish version.
2. Tell students, "Name all of the kinds of bugs you can think of." As students name the bugs, list them on a chart. List insects separately from arachnids and talk about the differences between them, such as different numbers of legs, different numbers of body parts, etc.
3. Copy the bug pictures on heavy paper and label them: *praying mantis, ladybug, yellow jacket, ant, cricket,* and *butterfly.* Then, list the Spanish names for these insects on separate index cards: *mantis religiosa, mariquita, avispa, hormiga, grillo,* and *mariposa.* Let students match the cards to the pictures.

Related Literature

- *About Bugs* by Sheryl Scarborough (Treasure Bay, Inc., 1998)
- *Bugs! Bugs! Bugs!* by Jennifer Dussling (Dorling Kindersly, 1999)
- *The Icky Bug Alphabet Book* by Jerry Palotta (Charlesbridge, 1987)

Translation Notes

Bugs on parade is translated here as *Parade of bugs.*

Bugs can be so colorful is translated as *How many colors the insects have!*

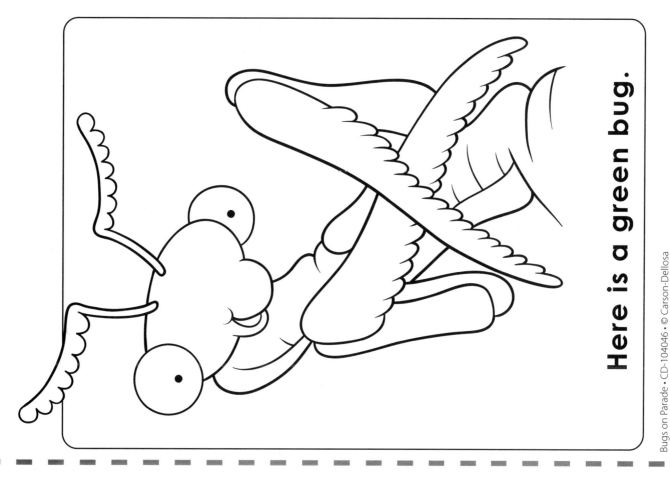

Here is a green bug.

Bugs on Parade

Written by Susan M. Ketch

Illustrated by Wayne Miller

Here is a yellow bug.

Here is a red and black bug.

Here is a black bug.

Here is a red bug.

Bugs can be so colorful.

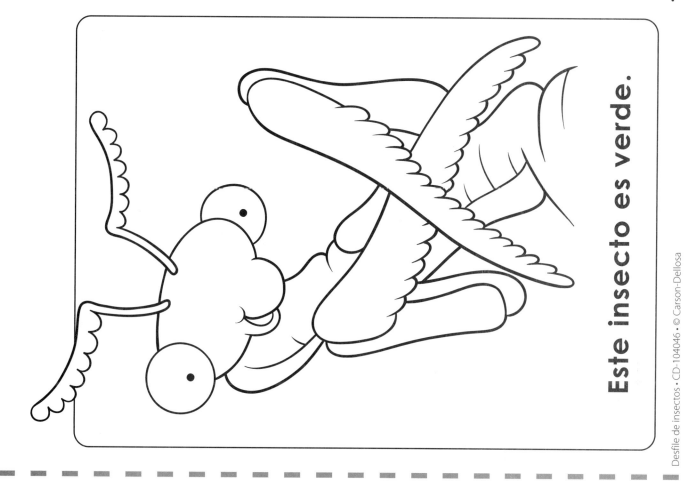

Este insecto es verde.

Desfile de insectos

Escrito por Susan M. Ketch

Ilustrado por Wayne Miller

Este insecto es amarillo.

Este insecto es rojo y negro.

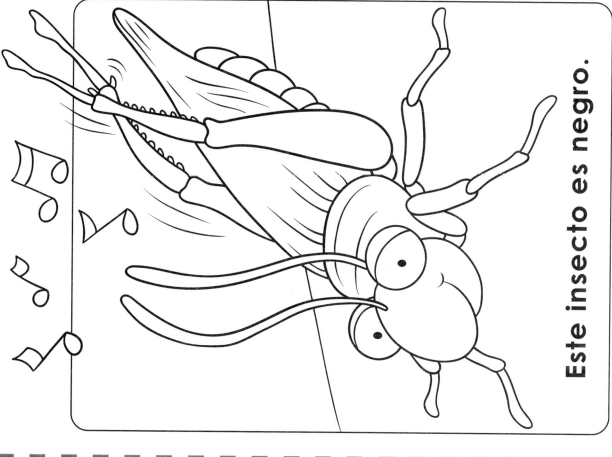

Este insecto es negro.

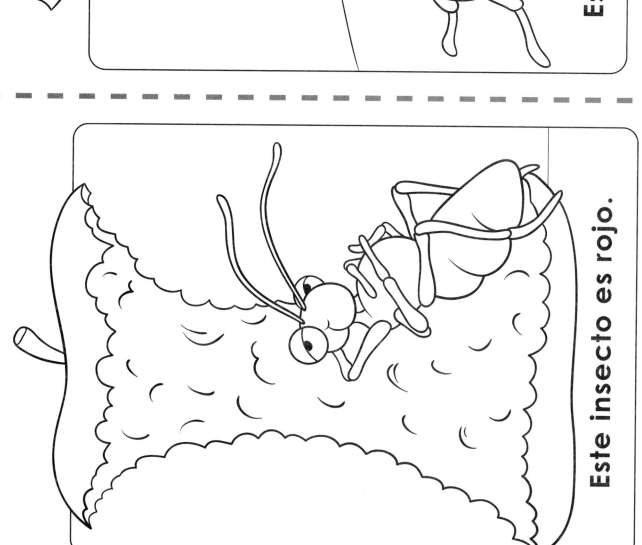

Este insecto es rojo.

¡Cuántos colores tienen los insectos!

Desfile de insectos • CD-104046 • © Carson-Dellosa

Quack, Duck, Quack!

Craig Johnson

Level 4

Number of English Words: 65

Number of Spanish Words: 76

Pre-Reading Activities

Book Introduction: This book tells about animals that try to teach a duck to quack.

Discussion Suggestions: Ask, "Can animals teach each other to make the "right" sounds? What kinds of sounds do animals make? When animals make sounds, do you think they are talking?"

Picture Walk: As you show the pictures, ask students to name the different types of animals.

Word Work:
Punctuation—Identify quotation marks and exclamation points.
Sight words—Students should learn to sight read *he, like,* and *to.*
Word analogies—Compare the ending sounds and spellings of the words *duck* and *quack.* Also compare the ending sounds and spellings of the words *gato, pato, perro, dijo, pero, patito, pavo,* and *cerdo.*
Structure—Point out that *The _____ said (to the duck)* and *le dijo al pato* are recurring patterns, as are *Quack, duck, quack!* and *¡Di cuac, patito!*

Post-Reading Activities

1. Let students make the animal sound for each animal pictured.

2. Ask, "Can you think of some animals that do not make sounds? How do they communicate?"
3. Let pairs teach each other how to do things, like tie shoes, whistle, etc.

Independent Activities

1. Have students try to sound-spell different animal noises.
2. Post pictures of farm animals. Let students study them and then ask students to close their eyes. Remove a picture. Ask students to open their eyes and try to name the missing picture.
3. Create a farm scene on a bulletin board and let students create animals from construction paper to place on the board.

Related Literature

- *Click Clack Moo: Cows That Type* by Doreen Cronin (Simon & Schuster, 2000)
- *The Little Red Hen* edited by Diane Muldrow (Golden Books, 2001)
- *Make Way for Ducklings* by Robert McCloskey (Viking, 1941)

Translation Notes

The sentence *The duck did not quack* is translated as *But the duck said nothing.* Note that the phrase *no dijo nada* is a double-negative and is correct in Spanish.

Little Stories for Little Readers • CD-104046

Quack,
Duck,
Quack!

Written by Craig Johnson

Illustrated by Ray Lambert

The cat said to the duck, "Quack, duck, quack!"

The duck did not quack.

The dog said, "Quack, duck, quack!"

The duck did not quack.

The turkey said to the duck, "Quack, duck, quack!"

The duck did not quack.

The pig said, "Quack, duck, quack!"

The duck did not quack.

The duck said to the duck, "Quack, duck, quack!"

The duck said, "Quack, quack, quack!"

¡Di cuac, patito!

Escrito por Craig Johnson

Ilustrado por Ray Lambert

El gato le dijo al pato: —¡Di cuac, patito!

Pero el pato no dijo nada.

El perro le dijo al pato: —¡Di cuac, patito!

Pero el pato no dijo nada.

El pavo le dijo al pato:—¡Di cuac, patito!

Pero el pato no dijo nada.

El cerdo le dijo al pato: —¡Di cuac, patito!

Pero el pato no dijo nada.

El pato le dijo al pato: —¡Di cuac, patito!

Y el pato dijo: —¡Cuac, cuac, cuac!

I Live on a Farm

Craig Johnson

Level 4
Number of English Words: 82
Number of Spanish Words: 72

Pre-Reading Activities

Book Introduction: In this book, a boy tells about the numbers and colors of animals and other things on his farm.

Discussion Suggestions: Ask, "Do you live on farms? Would you like to live on farms? Have you ever been to a farm? Can you name any farm animals?"

Picture Walk: As you show the pictures, have students name the different types of animals.

Word Work:
Sight vocabulary—Students should learn to sight read *on* and *my* and possibly number and color words.
Structure—Point out that *On my farm, there are* _____ is a recurring pattern. Also note the pattern found in *En mi granja hay* _____.

Post-Reading Activities

1. Have students write about and draw farms they would like to live on.
2. Talk about what things in the story could be different colors. Ask, "Are trees always green? Are cows always black and white?"
3. Let students find equivalent numbers of things in the classroom, such as one clock, two doors, three pieces of chalk, etc.

Independent Activities

1. Program a set of index cards with color and number words, or with English and Spanish words. Let students match them at a center according to the book.
2. Have students leave their book pages unstapled and sort them into categories, such as animals, plants, size, etc.
3. Help students add the number of things on each page (1 + 2 + 3, etc.). The total number is 55.

Related Literature

- *The Milk Makers* by Gail Gibbons (Aladdin, 1987)
- *Old MacDonald Had a Farm* by Carol Jones (Scholastic, 1994)
- *The Rusty, Trusty Tractor* by Joy Cowley (Boyd's Mills Press, 1999)

Translation Notes

Compare an English and Spanish phrase, such as *one blue pond* and *una laguna azul*. Explain that in English, describing words (*blue*) come before what they are describing (*pond*). But in Spanish, describing words (*azul*) come after what they are describing (*laguna*).

Little Stories for Little Readers • CD-104046

I Live on a Farm

Written by Craig Johnson

Illustrated by Erik Huffine

On my farm, there is one blue pond.

On my farm, there are two green hills.

On my farm, there are three brown goats.

On my farm, there are four black and white cows.

On my farm, there are five yellow ducks.

On my farm, there are six pink pigs.

On my farm, there are seven purple flowers.

On my farm, there are eight orange pumpkins.

On my farm, there are nine red chickens.

On my farm, there are ten white eggs.

Vivo en la granja

Escrito por Craig Johnson

Ilustrado por Erik Huffine

En mi granja hay una laguna azul.

En mi granja hay dos cerros verdes.

En mi granja hay tres cabras cafés.

En mi granja hay cuatro vacas blancas y negras.

En mi granja hay cinco patos amarillos.

En mi granja hay seis cerdos rosados.

En mi granja hay siete flores moradas.

En mi granja hay ocho calabazas anaranjadas.

En mi granja hay nueve pollos rojos.

En mi granja hay diez huevos blancos.

Coach Webb's House

Craig Johnson

Pre-Reading Activities

Book Introduction: Coach Webb has everything at her house for a baseball game, including players.

Discussion Suggestions: Ask, "What are your favorite sports? Have you ever played or watched baseball? What kind of equipment do you need to play baseball?"

Picture Walk: As students look at the pictures, let them try to explain how they know that the game being played is baseball and not another sport.

Word Work:
Sight vocabulary—Students should learn to sight read *has, at,* and number words. Structure—Point out that *Coach Webb has _____ at her house* and *En casa de la maestra Pérez* are recurring patterns.

Post-Reading Activities

1. Ask students to explain why the children went to Coach Webb's house and what other games they might have played there.
2. Practice throwing and catching with students and let each student hit a few balls from a T-ball tee.
3. Provide several types of sports balls. Let students name each kind of ball and tell what they know about the sport.

Independent Activities

1. Have each student tell a partner about a time when he played a game with an adult.
2. At a center, let each student practice writing the numerals and number words for one through ten. Then, let them point out which numbers are in the story.
3. Let students list all of the sports they can think of, then compare lists to see if they can add more.

Related Literature

- *Play Ball, Amelia Bedelia* by Peggy Parrish (HarperTrophy, 1995)
- *Take Me Out to the Ballgame* by Alec Gillman (Aladdin, 1999)
- *This Is Baseball* by Margaret Blackstone (Owlet, 1997)

Translation Notes

The word *maestra* is usually translated as *teacher. Entrenadora* is the typical word for *coach,* but it is a very long word for this reading level.

Webb is changed to *Pérez* to expose students to a traditional Hispanic name.

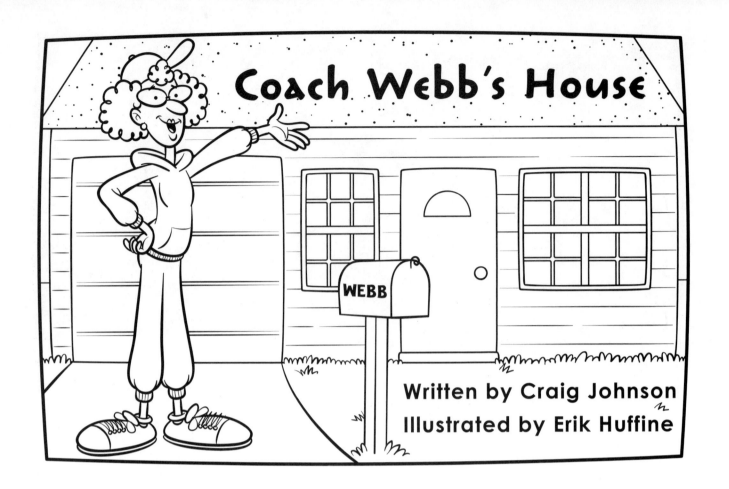

Coach Webb's House

Written by Craig Johnson
Illustrated by Erik Huffine

Coach Webb has one ball at her house.

Coach Webb has two bats at her house.

Coach Webb has three gloves at her house.

Coach Webb has four boys and five girls at her house.

Coach Webb has a baseball game at her house!

En casa de la maestra Pérez

Escrito por Craig Johnson

Ilustrado por Erik Huffine

En casa de la maestra Pérez hay una pelota.

En casa de la maestra Pérez hay dos bates.

En casa de la maestra Pérez hay tres guantes.

En casa de la maestra Pérez hay cuatro niños y cinco niñas.

¡En casa de la maestra Pérez hay un partido de béisbol!

School Stuff

Susan M. Ketch

Level 4
Number of English Words: 51
Number of Spanish Words: 33

Pre-Reading Activities

Book Introduction: The little girl in this book has a new backpack. She puts all of her new school supplies in her new backpack.

Discussion Suggestions: Ask, "Do you get new school supplies before school starts? Do you get new clothes? What new things do you like to get for school? What is the hardest thing to choose?"

Picture Walk: Ask students to identify the different items the girl puts into her backpack.

Word Work:
Sight words—Students should learn to sight read *put*, *new*, *in*, and *it*.
Word analogies—Compare the sounds in the words *it* and *in*.
Structure—Point out that *I put a new _____ in it* is a recurring pattern. The word *guardo* repeats in the Spanish version.

Post-Reading Activities

1. Ask, "Do you have some of the same items as the little girl? What are they?"
2. Have students name other things they could put in backpacks for school.
3. The teddy bear is an old friend. Ask students why they think the little girl wanted to put it in her new backpack.

4. Consider letting students bring in their favorite stuffed toys for show-and-tell.

Independent Activities

1. Have students make lists from memory of what they have in their backpacks.
2. Have students design and draw new backpacks that are large enough and have enough pockets to hold all of their stuff.
3. *Stuff* is a word that can mean several things. Talk about the noun and verb meanings. Have students write or dictate sentences using the word both ways. Also, explain that the Spanish word *cosas* means *things* and is not used as a verb.

Related Literature

- *If You Take a Mouse to School* by Laura Joffe Numeroff (Laura Geringer, 2002)
- *Miss Bindergarten Gets Ready for Kindergarten* by Joseph P. Slate (Aladdin, 1999)
- *Will I Have a Friend?* by Miriam Cohen (Aladdin, 1989)

Translation Notes

Compare the words *new* and *old* to the Spanish words *nuevo* and *viejo*.

Teach students the words *amigo* and *friend*. Talk about the differences between *amigos nuevos* and *amigos viejos*.

Little Stories for Little Readers • CD-104046

I have a new backpack.

School Stuff • CD-104046 • © Carson-Dellosa

School Stuff

Written by Susan M. Ketch

Illustrated by Erik Huffine

I put a new pencil in it.

I put a new lunch box in it.

I put new crayons in it.

I put lots of paper in it.

I put my old friend in it.

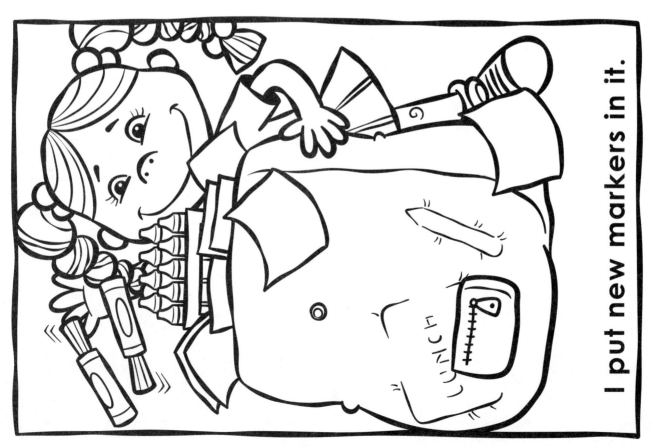

I put new markers in it.

I like my new backpack!

Tengo una mochila nueva.

Cosas de la escuela

Escrito por Susan M. Ketch

Ilustrado por Erik Huffine

Guardo mi lonchera nueva.

Guardo mi lápiz nuevo.

Guardo mis crayones nuevos.

Guardo muchos papeles.

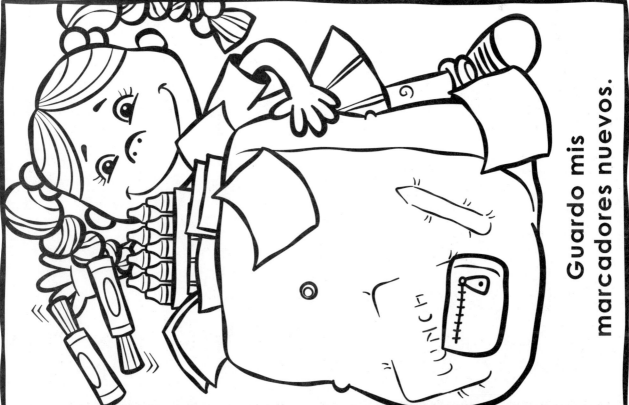

Guardo mis
marcadores nuevos.

Guardo a mi viejo amigo.

Cosas de la escuela • CD-104046 • © Carson-Dellosa

Cosas de la escuela • CD-104046 • © Carson-Dellosa

¡Me gusta mi mochila nueva!

Spiders

Susan M. Ketch

Level 4
Number of English Words: 40
Number of Spanish Words: 41

Pre-Reading Activities

Book Introduction: This story is about spiders.

Discussion Suggestions: Ask, "Where have you seen spiders? Many people are afraid of spiders, but they are very helpful to us. How do you think spiders might be helpful?"

Picture Walk: Point out the legs, body parts, and eyes of some of the spiders. Show the picture of a bug caught in a web and explain that spiders catch insects for food.

Word Work:
Sight words—Students should learn to sight read *have* and *can*.
Word analogies—Compare the sounds of the words *do* and *to*.

Post-Reading Activities

1. Ask students, "Can you think of another creature with eight legs? It lives in the ocean." Some students will be able to name the octopus.
2. Tell students to name two things they learned about spiders.
3. Practice web weaving with students. Stand in a circle and hold the end of a ball of yarn. Toss the ball to a student. Have him hold the strand and toss the ball to another student. Repeat twice with all students. Let an adult volunteer photograph the web, then let students unravel it in reverse order.

Independent Activities

1. At a center, let students use yarn and glue to make individual spiderwebs by gluing the yarn to heavy paper. Then, let students add spiders made from pom-poms and chenille craft sticks.
2. Tell students to search for spiders the next time they are outside. Suggest that they look under the playground equipment or near lights. Tell them to be kind and not touch the spiders.
3. Let each student write three reasons he likes or dislikes spiders.

Related Literature

• *The Itsy Bitsy Spider* by Iza Trapani (Charlesbridge, 1998)
• *Miss Spider's Tea Party: The Counting Book* by David Kirk (Scholastic, 1997)
• *The Very Busy Spider* by Eric Carle (Philomel, 1995)

Translation Notes

Telaraña is the word for *spiderweb*. *Tela* by itself can mean *cloth* or *fabric*, among other things.

Lampara araña means *chandelier*.

Spiders have eight legs.

Spiders • CD-104046 • © Carson-Dellosa

Spiders

Written by Susan M. Ketch

Illustrated by Wayne Miller

Spiders can have eight eyes.

Spiders have two main body parts.

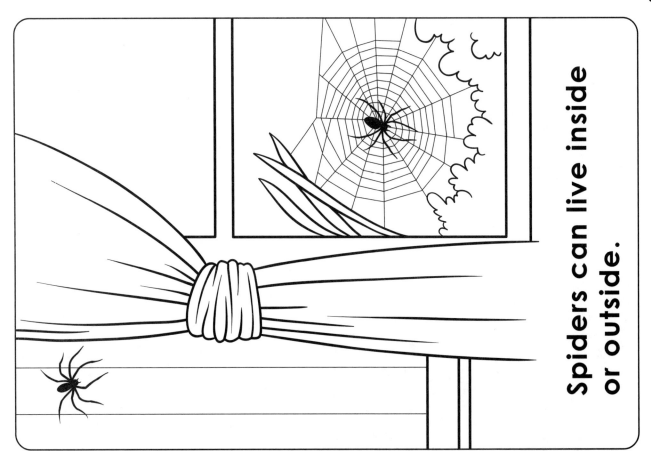

Some spiders make
webs to catch bugs.

Spiders can live inside
or outside.

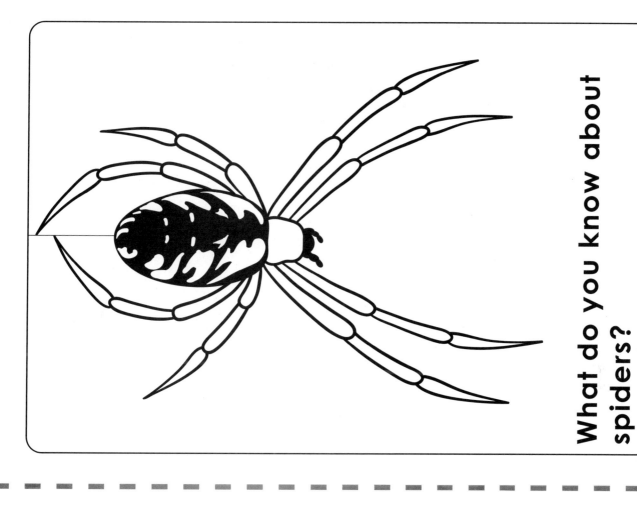

What do you know about spiders?

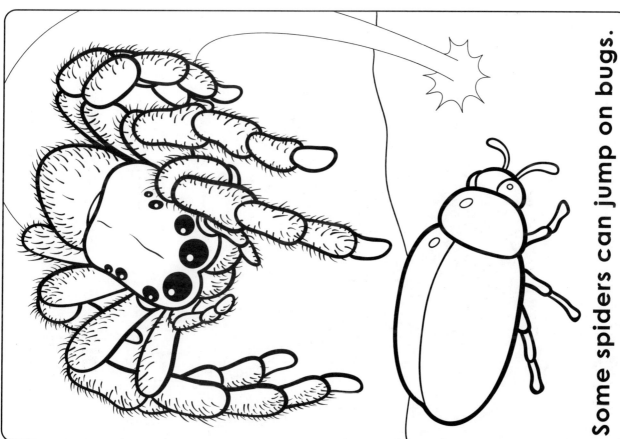

Some spiders can jump on bugs.

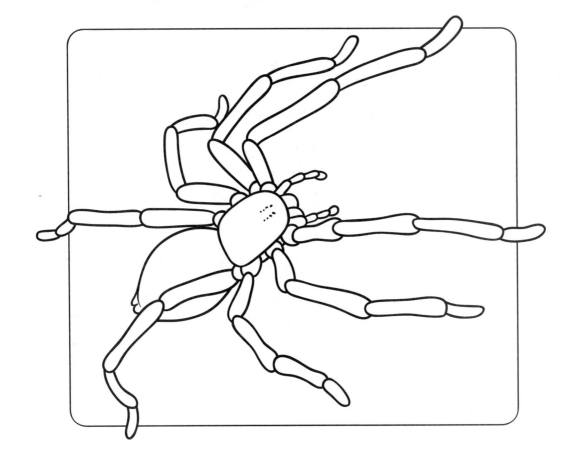

Las arañas tienen ocho patas.

Las arañas • CD-104046 • © Carson-Dellosa

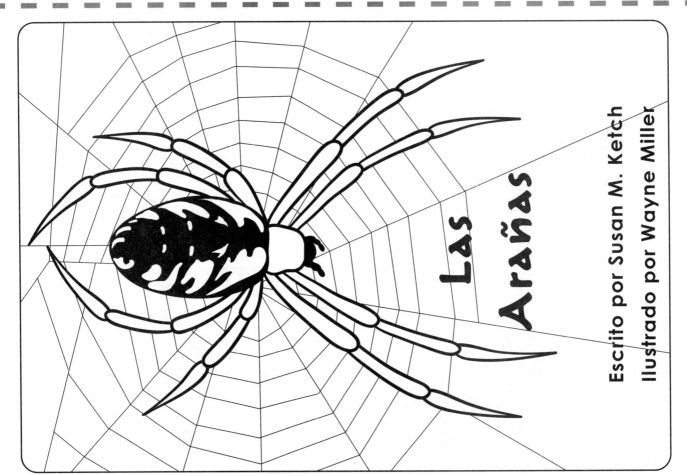

Las Arañas

Escrito por Susan M. Ketch

Ilustrado por Wayne Miller

Las arañas pueden
tener ocho ojos.

Su cuerpo tiene dos
partes principales.

Unas arañas hacen telarañas para atrapar insectos.

Las arañas viven dentro o afuera.

¿Qué sabes de las arañas?

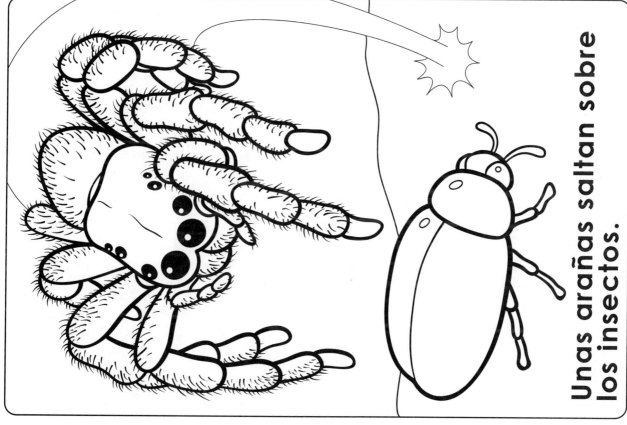

Unas arañas saltan sobre los insectos.

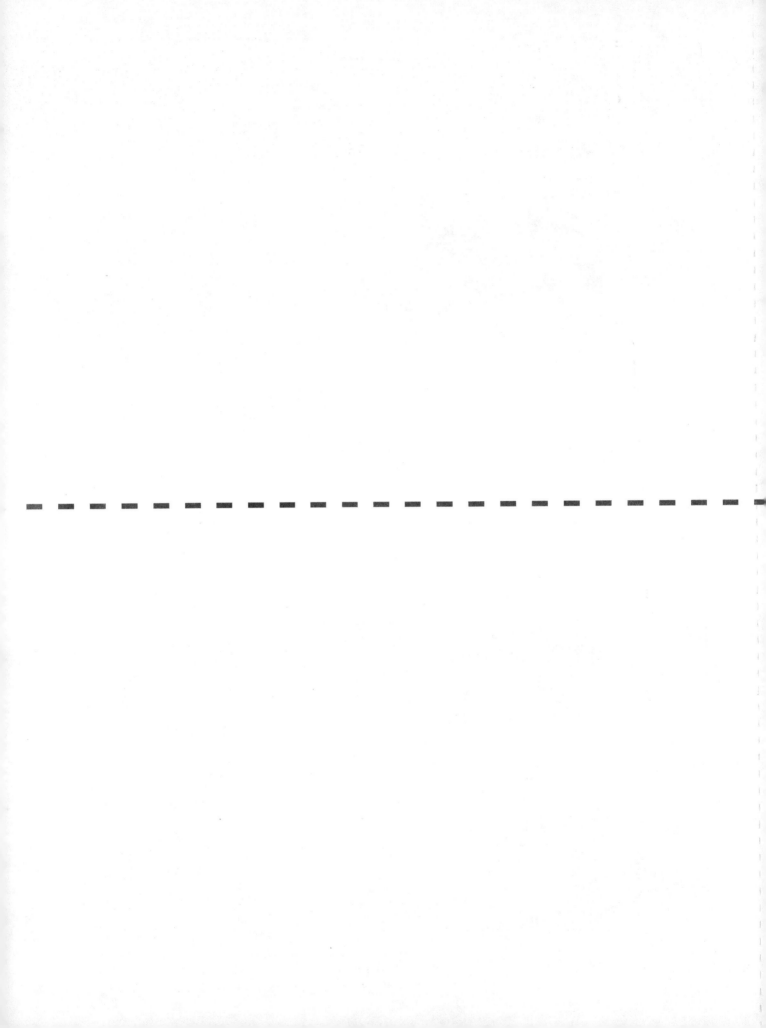

Good Work, Little Reader!

_____

student's name

_____

date

¡Buen trabajo, estudiante brillante!

_____

student's name

_____

date

Glossary

Title Pages:
escrito por written by
ilustrado por illustrated by

Let's Eat Ice Cream & ¡Qué rico helado!:
a to (has many meanings, most are preposition words like to, of, in, on)
Abuelita Grandmother (literally, little grandmother, granny)
Abuelito Grandfather (literally, little grandfather, grampa)
comer to eat
dijo said
gusta like
heladería ice cream shop
helado ice cream
Mamá mom
nos us
Papá dad
qué how (when used in exclamations)
rico delicious (can also mean rich)
sí yes
todos all
vamos let's go

Be Nice to Animals & Cuida los animales:
al to the (a + el)
animales animals
conejo/conejito rabbit/little rabbit (-ito used as an ending to indicate affection)
cuida look after, take care of (similar to "be nice")
cuídalos Let's take care of
gato/gatito cat/little cat (-ito used as an ending to indicate affection)
muchos a lot
pájaro/pajarito bird/little bird (-ito used as an ending to indicate affection)
perro/perrito dog/little dog (-ito used as an ending to indicate affection)
pez/pececito fish/little fish (-ito used as an ending to indicate affection)
todos all
un one/a
veo I see

Don't Make a Mess, Tess! & ¡Consuelo, no tires las cosas al suelo!:
al on the (a + el)
¡ay! Oops! Alas! Woe is me!
cosas things
dijeron they said
dijo he/she said
hermana sister
hermano brother
las the
mamá mom
me me
mi my
no don't (as it is used here)
papá dad
suelo floor
tiré threw
tires throw
No tires las cosas al suelo. together, means "Do not throw things on the floor."
todos everybody
ya already

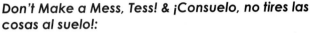

My New Puppy & Mi perrito:
aquí here
cordón cord, rope
del on the (de + el)
dormido asleep
divertido fun
el the
es is
está is
jabón soap
mi my
muerde bites
muy very
perrito little dog (Cachorrito is the word for puppy, but perrito is used here to make the rhyme better.)
pipí wet (the floor)
se come eats
se hace makes
tira pulls
ya already

Scribbles & Garabato:

a at (can also mean to, of, in, on)
beber to drink
comer to eat
cobaya guinea pig
dormir to sleep
en in
es is
garabato doodle, scribble
gusta likes
jugar to play
le him (indirect object)
les them (indirect object)
los the (plural)
mi my
niños children
salón classroom
un a
ver to see
vive lives

Weather & El tiempo:

alboroto tumultuous (used for messy)
cada each
calor hot or heat
con with
de of
día day
días days
diferente different
el the
es is (it is)
frío cold
hay there are
lindo pretty
lluvioso rainy
mojado wet
nieve snow
nublado cloudy
oscuro dark
qué how (used with exclamations)
soleado sunny
tiempo weather (often means time)
un a
viento wind
y and

Bugs on Parade & Desfile de insectos:

amarillo yellow
colores colors
cuántos how many (used as an exclamation)
es is
este this
insecto insect
insectos insects
los the
negro black
rojo red
tienen they have
verde green
y and

Quack, Duck, Quack! & ¡Di cuac, patito!:

al to the (a + el)
cuac quack
cerdo pig
di say
dijo said
el the
gato cat
le him (direct object)
nada nothing
no no
patito duckling
pato duck
pero but
perro dog
pavo turkey
y and

I Live on a Farm & Vivo en la granja:

amarillos yellow
anaranjadas orange
azul blue
blancas white
blancos white
cabras goats
cafés brown
calabazas pumpkins
cerdos pigs
cerros hills
cinco five
cuatro four
diez ten
dos two
en in/on
flores flowers
granja farm
hay there is/there are
huevos eggs
laguna pond
mi my
moradas purple
negras black
nueve nine
ocho eight
patos ducks
pollos chickens
rojos red
rosados pink
seis six
siete seven
tres three
una one
vacas cows
verdes green
y and

© Carson-Dellosa
Little Stories for Little Readers • CD-104046

Coach Webb's House & En casa de la maestra Pérez:
bates bats
béisbol baseball
casa house
cinco five
cuatro four
de of
deportes sports
dos two
en in
equipo equipment
guantes gloves
hay there are/there is
la the
maestra teacher (used as coach here)
niñas girls
niños boys
para for
partido game
pelota ball
tres three
un one
una one
y and

School Stuff & Cosas de la escuela:
a at
amigo friend
cosas things
crayones crayons
escuela school
guardo I keep or store
lápiz pencil
lonchera lunch box
me gusta I like
mi my
mis my
mochila backpack
muchos much
nueva new
nuevo new
nuevos new
papeles papers
marcadores markers
tengo I have
una one
viejo old

Spiders & Las arañas:
afuera outside
arañas spiders
atrapar to trap
cuerpo body
de about
dentro inside
dos two
hacen they make
insectos insects
las the
los the
o or
ocho eight
ojos eyes
para for
partes parts
patas legs
principales main
pueden they can
qué what
sabes you know
saltan they jump
sobre on
su its
telarañas webs
tener to have
tiene it has
tienen they have
unas some
viven they live

Teachers' Translation Note: Many Spanish adjectives change endings according to whether the nouns they modify are masculine or feminine, and singular or plural. For example, the common word for *new* is *nuevo*, but the translation for *new backpack* is *mochilla nueva*. The common word for *green* is *verde*, but the translation for *green hills* is *cerros verdes*. For ease of use, the words in this glossary are translated exactly as students will see them in the stories. Reteach common words as necessary.

Also, note that the Spanish verbs are listed exactly as they are conjugated in the stories. Therefore, if the different verb forms confuse English-speaking students, explain that just like English speakers use different verb forms with different pronouns (I jump, he jumps), Spanish speakers do the same (salto, salta). When teaching the Spanish verbs in isolation, concentrate on the infinitive forms.

Little Stories for Little Readers • CD-104046